The Battle is the Lord's

The Battle is The Lord's
Copyright © 2020 by Rebecca Starr Trammell
All rights reserved.

This book or any portion thereof may not be reproduced or used in any manner whatsoever without the express written permission of the author, except for brief quotations in a book review. Unless otherwise specified, Scripture quotations are from The King James Version of the Bible.

ISBN: 979-8-692-42955-1
First Printing, 2020, USA

Table of Contents

Foreword by Sara Starr Copple	5
Acknowledgements	8
Introduction	9
When Fear Starts… Faith Disappears	10
Simple Faith	14
Truth in the Inward Man	16
Carnally Minded	18
Spiritual Discipline	20
At the Right Hand of God	22
Love Not the World	24
Many are the Afflictions of the Righteous	26
Love Jesus More	28
You're Troubling the Man of God	31
The Door to Your Cabin is Wide Open	34
What Will it Take to Bring You to God?	36
David Recovered All	38
Energy Blend	40
Learn From Your Mistakes	42
A Wounded Spirit	44

Table of Contents

Everything Can Be Shaken	47
Waiting on God	49
Rejoice and Again I Say Rejoice	51
I am Covered by His Blood	53
No One Ever Cared for Me Like Jesus	55
Read the Fine Print	57
It Happened in the Furnace	60
I Belong to the King	62
He Knew How to Treat Others	64
Give Me a Miracle Mindset	66
The Love of Christ Compels Me	68
Sheltered in the Arms of God	70
It's Possible With God	72
Just and the Unjust	74
A Lion and a Pit	76
Conclusion: While You're Waiting	80

Foreword

"When you feel like the world is coming against you, take comfort knowing that the Lord will fight your battles for you."

I have grown up knowing Rebecca Trammell all of my life. We grew up in a pastor's home with parents who were both raised in ministry families. You experience a lot of living in that environment, and see into the real experiences of people's lives from birth to death when you work in a full-time healing profession. We lived lives of helping people through every situation in their day-to-day lives. We would support families and individuals in crisis and serve them in times of joy or sadness. I am Rebecca's baby sister and the youngest of the five Starr girls.

That means I have had a real, personal, front row seat to see her in each stage of her life. Rebecca has always been a natural born leader and a sought after trusted confidant. She has always been genuine in her love for all people, and her character has been one of caring for others. I have found her advice and listening ear has been a blessing to help guide me through life. She is known by those around her for being A light and stabilizing voice that can bring spiritual insight and strength during dark times. She comes along with her quiet strength when you need that strong foundation to help you carry on. She has been an example of thoughtfulness and sensitivity when it comes to speaking faith into others' lives in their time of brokenness.

Reading these chapters is a window into her personal insight through some of life's toughest blows. I have talked to her during those times and felt the heavy weight of those situations, and at the same time I've watched her lean on God. She would share with me a scripture verse that was instrumental in giving her the strength to face those obstacles. These devotional chapters are an extension of her voice and insight to you, and something you can read over and over in those times you need strength.

When she speaks on the "Battle is the Lord's," she is speaking from her own behind the scenes of her life journey. She has a testimony of being through some dark nights of the soul experiences, and yet she saw personal victory by cementing her faith in God's keeping power. I have seen her walk into any situation during her years in ministry and bring calm and peace from her place of prayer and faith.

She is someone you can trust to lift your thoughts higher than your current circumstances and human emotions, to give you a God perspective. She is slow to give out advice and opinions unless it is filtered through prayer, love, and wisdom from the Lord. She has been a seeker of truth, who practices balanced living and maintaining healthy relationships. I know that Rebecca is a woman of God at home, as well as in her public ministry where she travels all around the world with her husband Rev. David Trammell to minister and support other leaders. She has been a selfless daughter, sister, leader, friend, wife, mother, and grandmother. She is an exceptional speaker, pastor's wife, and student of the word. Rebecca has been the one we can trust with our life's most personal needs because she would turn to her prayer closet to get a word from the Lord. You know when she speaks it will come from a place of prayer and Godly wisdom.

Rebecca has always stood out as a sensitive heart, spiritual leader, always compassionate to others, and a constant settled security in our lives. I believe this book will be a blessing to all that pick it up.

Sara Starr Copple

Acknowledgements

I want to thank all those who helped me make this book a reality. My husband is my biggest fan and supporter, thank you David. Also my friend Anthony Miller, who has made this book possible. Without his expertise, this book would not have been completed.

Thank you to my sister Sara for her kind words in the foreword, my friend Betty Strawcutter who willingly takes on the job of proofreading my work, and my daughter Farrah who created my book cover.

Special thanks to my parents, although they have been deceased for many years their love, Godly guidance and teaching has been the foundation of my life.

Most of all, I give God the glory for his love and blessings on my life. Without Him, life would not be worth living.

                    Rebecca Starr Trammell

Introduction

And he said, Hearken ye, all Judah, and you inhabitants of Jerusalem, and thou King Jehoshaphat, thus says the Lord to you, Do not fear nor be dismayed because of this great multitude, for the battle is not yours but God's.
2 Chronicles 20:15 KJV

Day after day, my mind was trying to figure out where this particular trial came from, and what caused it. No matter how long I thought about this problem, all I ended up with was confusion.

I got so tired of thinking about this situation that I cried out to God and said, *"Lord, help me get past this problem! I don't know what to do or how to act."*

Then the Lord impressed me with these words: *The Battle is the Lord's*. I picked up my Bible to look it up, and began to see what God was trying to tell me. As I studied the Old Testament, I read about what happened to Judah. I realized I wasn't the first of God's people going through a trial they couldn't win on their own.

So every time those thoughts began to trouble me, my battle cry became: *The Battle is the Lord's*.

I don't know when that trial quit bothering me. As I proclaimed *The Battle is the Lord's,* my enemy disappeared. Thank you Lord for answering your people when they call out to you! One more victory I can declare as I testify of your goodness.

What is something the Lord has already done in your life? Write it out and thank Him below.

Where Fear Starts... Faith Disappears

*I sought the Lord, and he heard me,
and delivered me from all my fears.*
Psalm 34:4 KJV

I was staying the night in a foreign country, when something woke me up at night. I realized it was my toe hurting. When I looked at it, I became instantly afraid, it was angry red and looked very infected.

The fear washed over me like waves. I thought about the fact that this had always been something I never wanted to happen... to be sick in a foreign country and have need of a hospital. What I had read a few days before came to mind: *when fear begins, faith stops.* I grabbed ahold of that thought and texted a prayer partner back in the States, asking her to pray for me. Then I said to God, *"You can take care of this."*

I took a Tylenol and an antibiotic and the next thing I knew, I woke up from a good night's sleep!

I felt better the next day, but God was still looking out for me. It was a Sunday, and a friend from home who's a nurse texted me to let me know she wouldn't be at church that morning. I let her know that I was out of the country, but that I'd pass her message along.

Then I sent her a picture of my toe and let her know what had happened. She was concerned that it looked very serious, told me I needed a stronger antibiotic, and that I shouldn't wait till I got home. I told her that I would try, if God worked it out, to get the proper antibiotic. After service, I asked the missionary if we could go to a pharmacy and see if they would give me the right antibiotic. He felt doubtful, but was willing to try for his guest. I made my husband go in with me, in case a man's presence would make more of an impression.

I showed the pharmacist the picture of my angry toe, and said my health person at home said a certain antibiotic was what I needed, and in less then 5 minutes I walked out with it!

The pharmacist informed us that he did not usually do that, but that he would do that for me. I thought, *"Wow, God! It's amazing how quick you can handle a situation."*

I have rejoiced every time I have thought of this. God has no limitations. I do my best every time fear strikes to stop it, and replace it with faith.

We have an awesome miracle worker in God!

Write out a time when God worked quickly on your behalf, providing something or protecting you from something. Recall how you felt when He came through for you.

Simple Faith

For with God nothing shall be impossible. God gives us a promise in his word, that if we pray, He hears.
Luke 1:37 KJV

Whatever need you can have, whatever problem you are up against as you read this book, call out to God in *simple faith* that he hears you. I love the joy of praying in secret about a situation and seeing God answer openly. I have a secret weapon! When you learn how to pray the prayer of faith, nothing in your life will be impossible with God. Go through your day praying for whatever needs you encounter. Requests, prayers, intercession, and thanksgiving can be made for everyone. Even if you don't know someone personally, but you pass their way and witness a need, pray for them.

Pray with faith daily for our country, president, leaders of our community, all those that are in authority, and last but not least, the Pastors and leaders in our churches. That we will live peaceful, quiet lives in godliness and holiness. This is God's desire. He loves everyone and wants all men to be saved by coming to the saving knowledge
of the Truth.

For there is one God, and one mediator between God and men, the man Christ Jesus;
1 Timothy 2:5 KJV

Write out your prayers for our country, president, leaders of our community, all those that are in authority, and last but not least, the Pastors and leaders in our churches. Thank God for their service and ask Him to move on their behalf.

_____

_____

_____

_____

_____

_____

_____

_____

_____

_____

_____

_____

_____

_____

Truth in the Inward Man

Behold thou desireth truth in the inward; and in the hidden part thou shalt make me to know wisdom.
Psalm 51:6 KJV

Only God can keep us right in our thinking, our actions, and our living. Being right with God takes desire and discipline as you line up to His word. When we get off track in our ways, which we will as long as we are on this earth, we have to be quick to cry out to God. We must ask Him for forgiveness and to cleanse our mind, heart, and actions. God is willing and able to help us, yet it takes desire to humble ourselves in order to confess our sin and ask forgiveness.

The psalm above was written by David. You may know that the Bible says David was a man after God's own heart. This was true even though he sinned. Reading through the scriptures that documented his life, we can see that he sinned miserably. In spite of sin, he had enough faith in God that when he was at his worst, that he would cry out for God to forgive him and cleanse him. Because of this desire to stay right in his thoughts, actions, and his living, God could simply not overlook the faith he continuously displayed.

Examine your recent thoughts, actions, and living. Have these areas of your life glorified God, or have you become distracted by the cares of this world? Ask God to search your heart and mind, bring sinful things to light, and ask forgiveness.

Carnally Minded

For to be carnally minded is death; but to be spiritually minded is life and peace. Because the carnal mind is enmity against God: for it is not subject to the law of God, neither indeed can be. So then they that are in the flesh cannot please God.
Romans 6:6-8

To be carnally minded is to center your thoughts and feelings on yourself. You may say you love God, but ask yourself, do you line yourself to God's Word? Are your actions and reactions lined up to what God says to do? When something happens and you think of the Godly way to respond, but inside your human spirit, feelings are welling up and trying to take over, the carnal mind is warring against Godly actions. If you seriously want a spiritual mind, it is times like that where you need to slow down and ask God through prayer and the Word, to give you the strength to what is right in His sight, not based on how you feel, and how you want to respond. This spiritual way is real, but you have to be sold out to God, and really want to respond His way. It will take daily prayer, reading the Word, and vigilance to be spiritually minded. It's a daily walk of faith.

Truly holding on to your touch of God is more important than what happens to you or around you. The intentional decision to be spiritually minded is well worth it.

Reflect on ways you may have unintentionally or intentionally allowed yourself to be carnally minded. Pray and ask God to help you realign yourself to Him, His Word, and His desire for your life.

Spiritual Discipline

But I have prayed for thee, that thy faith fail not: and when thou art converted, strengthen thy brethren.
Luke 22:32

There's never a day you don't need to pray. We are bombarded with things daily that can offend us and make us bitter. You have got to be like a non-stick skillet by not letting any offense stick to you. Your salvation is too important, and we are to close to our reward, to let things stick. One thing I have found out in my life time is that the devil will use whatever it takes to get me off track.

If bitterness or offense will work to distract you and tear you down, he will make sure many things come your way to accomplish his goal to steal, kill, and destroy. You have to be vigilant. If bitterness and offense will take you down. The devil is happy. That works for him. Don't let it stick to you.

Keep praying, keep fasting, and keep reading the Word. Be serious about your walk with God. Your walk with God will be a source of strength to others.

Similarly, backsliding is the cancer of Christianity. It discourages those around you that look to you for hope and help.

Consider your recent spiritual discipline in regards to praying, fasting, and reading the Word of God. In which ways can you improve this area of your life? Pray for a fresh desire to seek God's face.

_____

_____

_____

_____

_____

_____

_____

_____

_____

_____

_____

_____

_____

At the Right Hand of God

Looking unto Jesus the author and finisher of our faith; who for the joy that was set before him endured the cross, despising the shame, and is set down at the right hand of God
Hebrews 12:2 KJV

In our walk with God there are bound to be *things* that happen. Just because we are Christians does not mean that we will not be targeted by the enemy. In fact, the opposite is true! Discouragement, fears, and strange trials will come into our lives.

The same things that happen to unbelievers happen to believers. The difference is that we know who to turn to - the author and finisher of our faith - the one true living God - Jesus Christ.

Be sure of your calling in God and of your salvation. In moments of trials, look to Jesus for comfort and peace, trust his leading, know that He knows all and sees all. Trust that there must be a need for this path, you remember that He knows the end from the beginning. Looking unto Jesus provides peace.

When I don't know what's going on or why things are happening, I know He does, because He has a plan. *"For I know the plans I have for you, declares the Lord. Plans to prosper you and not to harm you, plans to give you hope and a future."* Jeremiah 29:11

God uses His power to work His plan in your life. Think about recent challenges in your life, and write them out as you trust in God. Ask Him to renew your faith through your struggles. He knows and loves you.

Love Not the World

Love not the world, neither the things that are in the world. If any man love the world, the love of the father is not in him. For all that is in the world, the lust of the flesh, lust of my eyes, and the pride of life, is not of the father, but is of the world. And the world passeth away, and the lust thereof: but he that doeth the will of God abideth for ever.
1 John 2:15-17 KJV

This scripture has special significance in my life. My father was a hero to me. His love and allegiance to God was very noteworthy. He would quote this scripture in his teaching and in his prayers, and it got my attention. He was serious about serving God and pleasing God was the most important thing to him. As his child I watched and listened to him pray and that feeling was transferred to me. As a child I didn't understand what all those things signified, but as I grew in Christ as trials and tests came my way , I weighed it all out. One by one God gave me the strength to choose His way as this scripture says.

Praying the scriptures gives you power through the Spirit to handle any situation that comes your way. We have no power within ourselves to do the will of God, but it's His Spirit through us that is manifested as we walk uprightly before him. Daily devotions and prayer is a must to keep the Spirit working in our life. If you leave any space in your life, then the lust of the flesh, the lust of the eyes, and the pride of life will show up.

Consider the lust of the flesh, the lust of the eyes, and the pride of life. Have one or more of these areas been a challenge for you lately? Reflect on this below and ask God's help in overcoming what is bothering you.

Many are the Afflictions of the Righteous

*Many are the afflictions of the righteous:
but the Lord deliver them out of them all.*
Psalms 34:19 KJV

A while ago, I was praying for a beloved friend that has faced many physical problems. God spared his life, but once again, he faced a set back. It seemed like he was caught in the "one step forward, one step back" routine. As I interceded for him, I asked God, *"Why does this continue to happen?" Just tell me why! Can't this friend just be well, and his sickness be totally gone?"* Then this scripture came to my mind: *Many are the afflictions of the righteous. But God delivers us out of them all.*

Believing in God and living righteously will not keep us from trouble and suffering in this life. Commitment to God sometimes brings testing and persecution. God has ordained that through many tribulations we must enter the kingdom of God. The suffering of the righteous must be endured with the knowledge that God desires to deliver us out of them. Either by supernatural intervention in this life, or victorious death. God gets a lot of glory when we suffer, but we have to hold onto our trust in Him. It's a testimony that speaks to many, and causes them to know that God is real. When a person suffers, yet keeps a good attitude and love for God, it makes others know that God's power is real. It's not something we can do ourselves, but only through the power of God that works in us.

Do you know someone who is battling an ongoing problem that just won't break? Write out a prayer for them below for strength, peace, and a desire to remain fully trusting in God through their trial. Call them or send a text to let them know you're praying for them.

_____

_____

_____

_____

_____

_____

_____

_____

_____

_____

_____

_____

Love Jesus More

*Jesus said unto him, Thou shalt love the Lord thy God
with all thy heart, and with all thy soul,
and with all thy mind.*
Matthew 22:37 KJV

I read a statement one time that said, "You love your spouse best when you love Jesus more". This profound statement impacted me after I read it. If you want to have a lasting marriage, the easiest way to do that is to love Jesus more. When you love Jesus more, through every adjustment and every difficulty, you can have Gods guidance, peace and help.

When we are following the Lord and have times in marriage where we think we are not being loved properly, not cared for like we want, not receiving the intimacy we desire, we can get those needs filled through our relationship with Jesus Christ. No man or woman can fully fill the needs in our life. We can do life together, we can raise a family together, but only God can satisfy our innermost beings.

You can put your hope in Jesus Christ and you can communicate to him every thought, every hurt, every need, every desire in secret and watch him work in your life openly. No husband or wife can listen to all these things I listed. We may want to, but we are not God and do not have the capacity to receive these things. Only our savior can. He listens, He speaks, and He guides us through prayer and His words. He makes us feel confident and secure enough to love another individual with a Godly love. This Godly love will keep us stable in the ups and downs of a relationship.

You should not consider yourself an empty vessel waiting for someone to fill it up, nor should you spend your life trying to fill up another human being. Only God can meet needs and fill voids in hearts.

It is very evident for marriage relationships to be successful, both people must love God the most. This sign is evident in successful marriages because their relationship flourishes due to having a Godly love and strength to impart to each other. If you don't love God the most, try it and see how your marriage can become all that you want it to be. You love your spouse the best... when you love Jesus the most.

If you're married, take some time to reflect on your marriage and compare its priority to your relationship with God. Weigh it out - are you loving your spouse most or are you loving Jesus most? The point is not to ignore the needs of your spouse, but to learn to be fulfilled through Christ and through your spouse. Pray that you and your spouse would love Jesus most.

If you're single, take some time to reflect on a Godly couple you know that loves Jesus most. In which ways is this evident? Pray for them that they would continue to do so. Are you loving Jesus the most in your current season of life? Are there other things taking your love first? Consider this and re-prioritize if necessary.

You're Troubling the Man of God

The thief cometh not, but for to steal, and to kill, and to destroy: I am come that they might have life, and that they might have it more abundantly.
John 10:10 KJV

God's man has to give an account for you. Why do you not seek to be absolved of your resentment, jealousy, bitterness? God's leadership is trying to help you, but you are hanging onto your issues, like a dog does an old bone. Sometimes it is your unresolved issues in the past that have resurfaced. Things you haven't taken care of in the past are taking on new forms and trying to grow new life in you again.

You have to be intentional about your life in Christ. The pastor stands by with baited breath, hoping that you will totally forgive and submit to God's leading. Not letting a root of bitterness go can cause many to be defiled.

Don't exclaim over some modern terror attacks, when you could snuff out several people's spiritual lives by your unresolved anger and bitterness. You have sought many friendships among the congregation and have those that look to you, and the enemy seeks to make you bitter so he can take many out of the congregation through you.

Though the pastor grieves, he cannot help you fully because you are not totally aware of the blood that will be on your hands from the people you have influenced. Many will wake up too late and realize what happened to them. They would like to seek God and return to Him, but they can't seem to make their way back through all the trouble and debris. When their life turns into shambles, they can't stand to take the blame, and point to the church leaders. They don't want to accept biblical authority to reprove, rebuke, and exhort, even though the goal is to help them. Scripture says, *"Whosoever conceals his transgressions will not prosper, but he who confesses and forsakes them will obtain mercy."* Proverbs 28:13

God helps those in leadership to handle the grieving of casualties in the house of God. The grief seems unbearable at times, because our Savior and Master said in His Word that He doesn't want anyone to perish. It is better to lift up holy hands without wrath or doubting.

Please don't be one of those that pass through the church on the way to hell.

After reading this devotion, take some time in prayer specifically over what was written here. Examine your own heart. Ask God to show you areas in your life where you're still holding onto bitterness, resentment, judgements, or anything else against another person, including your pastor and Church leadership. Write these areas out and allow this book to be a safe space for you as you release these things to God and out of your heart. Pray for your pastor and leadership, including their spouses, for supernatural strength and wisdom. Pray for yourself and others to be submitted to them as they follow Christ.

The Door to Your Cabin is Wide Open

Love not the world, neither the things that are in the world. If any man love the world, the love of the father is not in him. For all that is in the world, the lust of the flesh, lust of my eyes, and the pride of life, is not of the father, but is of the world. And the world passeth away, and the lust thereof: but he that doeth the will of God abideth for ever.
1 John 2:15-17 KJV

Our family went on a new adventure camping in rustic cabins and enjoying nature. I was so excited to be near nature that while I was setting up our cabin and making beds, I left the door wide open. While I was busy, I soon heard a scratching noise and look down to see an unknown animal, black in color, in the room with me, I am not very comfortable with animals. It turned out to be a neighboring cabin's pet bulldog, but it scared me so bad that for the rest of my stay, I kept my door closed. I used open windows for fresh air, but never opened the door.

Many people say they love God, but in the past have opened themselves up to lust of the flesh, lust of the eyes, and the pride of life. You need to take this time and search your soul. If you are struggling with unresolved issues, you have left your door open to your cabin. Though you say you love God, the enemy has easy access to your spirit through the open door. Once and for all seek deliverance from family curses, unresolved anger, and bitterness, so you may not only serve God, but enjoy the fruits of living for God: love, joy, peace, long suffering, gentleness, and meekness. Are there things in your past that you have not realized the seriousness of , and dealt with them through repentance? Do you have total deliverance so you may not just know about God but actually walk with God? Others will see and feel your Godly walk and gain strength and encouragement. Take inventory of your life and of your heart. What is God speaking to you?

What Will it Take to Bring You to God?

*Fall on the Rock, don't let the Rock fall
on you and grind you to powder.*
Matthew 21:44 KJV

God cares about us so much that he keeps trying to bring us back to Him. He desires for us to totally yield our lives, will, desires, our unresolved anger, hurts, and disappointments, so he can finally give us the desires He has for us.

Sometimes our will is so strong about something, we don't trust God. What will it take for you to finally yield all and submit your will and finally say,

"God, here is all my baggage for better or worse. I give it to you. Whatever You desire to do with me will be what's best for me. You're the boss." ?

When you have yielded all, then will you be able to start experiencing the joy in living. Will it always be easy? No, but you will feel the hand of the master each step of the way, knowing that He is with you in every situation to work it out for your good.

Are you still holding onto things that you have given to God only part-way? Are you still holding onto something so you can "check the progress" of it? Put your own will and desires in check and submit them to God. Jot down which areas of your life you need to do this in on the next page.

David Recovered All

And David recovered all that the Amalekites carried away: and David rescued his two wives. And there was nothing lacking to them, neither small nor great, neither sons nor daughters, neither spoil, nor any thing that they had taken to them: David recovered all.
1 Samuel 30:18-19 KJV

While David was away from his home the Amalekites raided, destroyed and took captives from his city, Ziklag. David determined to bring everything back. Even though he was faced with the tragedy of losing his family along with the families of his men, David wanted to recover their loss. His men though did not think about a plan of rescue, rather, they blamed David and wanted to kill him.

David turned to God for a solution—instead of looking for a scapegoat, and he found his strength and answer in Him. Remember when you have a "Ziklag Moment" don't be discouraged. Just as David's story didn't end there, neither does yours.

When troubles came to David he inquired of the Lord. What do you do when troubles come against you? What is your first reaction? Do you seek to blame others? Who is the scapegoat in your life? You can "recover it all" just like David did if you seek God for his solution, if you inquire of the Lord in prayer what your next step should be. Write out your prayer for God to change your reaction to things being "you focused" over to "God-focused."

Energy Blend

But those who hope in the Lord will renew their strength. They will soar on wings like eagles; they will run and not be weary, they shall walk and not faint.
Isaiah 40:31 KJV

I looked at a snack in my hand that was a mix of good seeds and fruits. It was proclaiming to be an energy blend, better known as a healthy snack.

God is my true energy blend. A very present help in time of trouble. Psalms 46:1 says *God is our refuge and strength, a very present help in trouble.* If my energy and strength is low it is because I have not spent the necessary time in His Word, in prayer, and in fasting. These three things make an awesome energy blend!

God does not leave his children without the strength to withstand the enemy, but it comes to us from a desire to have it. It takes effort and singleness of mind, looking unto Jesus, who is the author and finisher of our salvation.

Looking unto Jesus the author and finisher of our faith; who for the joy that was set before him endured the cross, despising the shame, and is set down at the right hand of the throne of God.
Hebrews 12:2

Have you been spending the necessary time reading, praying, and fasting as your supernatural energy blend? If not, repent and make a plan below to get yourself back on track.

_____

_____

_____

_____

_____

_____

_____

_____

_____

_____

_____

_____

_____

Learn From Your Mistakes

*If any man be in Christ, he is a new creature:
old things have passed away;
behold all things are become new.*
2 Corinthians 5:17   KJV

We all make mistakes in life - we are human! When those mistakes happen we may be embarrassed, defeated, hopeless, angry... all manner of emotions surface. However, through God and His Spirit working in us, nothing is impossible.

Mistakes can remind us that, within ourselves, we don't have the power to live an overcoming life. We must keep Him first, seeking His face daily. Our mistakes will be stepping stones for a greater, stronger, overcoming life in Him.

I have made mistakes both big and small in this life. We all have. Do not let your mistakes be justification for the enemy to convince you that you are not worthy of knowing your Savior. God loves us all in spite of our shortcomings, as we walk forward toward Him and strive to be like Him.

On the next page, walk back through a mistake you made maybe months or years ago. How did God use it as a teaching experience in your walk with Him? How could you have handled recovery from the mistake better? Did you fully trust in God for help? Pray that you remember in times of mistakes to lean on God.

A Wounded Spirit

*For if you forgive men their trespasses,
your Heavenly Father will also forgive you.*
Matthew 6:14   KJV

Consider this: when life deals you a hurtful blow, do you blame that hurt on a person or persons, then begin to nurse the hurt and let it grow within you like a cancer? Or do you take it to God in prayer, and continue to, until it's ugly hold starts to let go? A wounded spirit lives in a prison: it is held hostage by hurts and bitterness. It is difficult for other people to help those who hide in cells and keep the key with them.

You may have heard the saying that, *"Bitterness will hurt you more than the person you are bitter towards."* You will be the one to pay for it. They will go on. Most of the time the blow will hit in a place we are most tender at. The devil sees to that! This is not a person-to-person battle; this is the enemy of your soul, giving you a knock-out blow if he can. He never quits trying. He doesn't care what it takes to separate you from a life of peace and joy in the Holy Ghost. When your bitter spirit rears its ugly head showing others you are not healing by dealing with it through the power of the Holy Ghost, you begin to damage other relationships because your friends and family are not equipped to deal with a bitter spirit.

People may still love those with bitter spirits, but they have to do it from a distance. You will find yourself in solitary confinement with your bitterness.

You have the key to be free, but only God can help

you use it. Why not just follow the Bible way to and deal with the hurts and slights in this life? The Bible says if you don't forgive, I won't forgive you.

When ye stand praying, forgive, if ye have ought against any: that your Father also which is in heaven may forgive you of your trespasses.
Mark 11:25   KJV

Search your heart by taking several minutes in self-reflection, then ask God to begin to deal with you about any bitterness and unforgiveness. Maybe He will show you something you need to let go from years ago that you didn't even realize was still there. Only God can search your heart and soul and bring these things up.

Spend time in prayer before writing your reflection on the next page. What is God speaking to you?

...

Everything Can Be Shaken

*And this word, yet once more,
signifies the removing of those things that are shaken,
as of things that are made, that those things which
cannot shaken can remain.*
Hebrews 12:27   KJV

Trust me, there will be times when you feel surefooted and rock-solid in your faith in God, and then a problem or situation will come like a landslide and hit you full force. It can even happen right after God has spoken to you in a powerful way. You feel more faith than you ever have before, and have excitement for what God wants to accomplish through you. Then something hits you.

After you recover from the shock, I hope it knocks you to your knees in prayer so the enemy will not get an unfair advantage over you. God must have something special planned for you if the enemy wants to destroy your faith before God can fulfill His promises in your life, showing the world His power through you. As you recover, just remain rock-solid in your faith, so that the promises of God over your life can be fulfilled.

It's easy when things come against us to have a knee-jerk reaction to either solve the problem yourself, or start worrying. Has this happened to you Remember a time you've done this and ask forgiveness from God for not going to Him first.

Waiting on God

*The Lord is good unto them that wait for Him,
to the soul that seeketh Him.*
Lamentations 3:25   KJV

Who you and I become while we are waiting is more important than what we are waiting for. Through the waiting, God transforms our character. Abram waited for God's promises and became Abraham, father of many nations. Sarai waited on God's promises, and became Sarah the mother of Isaac. Joseph became the second in command to pharaoh in Egypt, but only after waiting years in a prison for a crime he didn't commit.

Sometimes we desire to do things, and we can't imagine why God is telling us to wait. To our natural eye, everything feels like we should go ahead. But you have been told to wait, to stand still. Your next move is to decide this: Will you wait, even though you don't understand why you're being told that, or will you take matters in your own hands and proceed? If you proceed on your own timing, you will understand one day why you were told to wait. Our God has all knowledge: He knows what's ahead. He wants a smooth path and blessings for us along the way, but if we choose to take matters into our own hands, if we are not sensitive or do not seek God's voice, then we cannot experience all that God has intended for us along the way.

Recall an example of how you took "timing" into your own hands instead of waiting until you were sure it was God's "timing". How did it end up? How can you make changes so that you trust that God's clock is correct in the future?

Rejoice and Again I Say Rejoice

Rejoice in the Lord always.
I will say it again: Rejoice!
Philippians 4:4   KJV

Troubles roll in like storm clouds and you stand looking toward the sky, speechless, without words to describe how you feel. In your heart, you say, *God, what now? What's coming next?* Then you hear that still small voice saying, *Rejoice! Again, I say rejoice.*

Obey and lift praises to God! Rejoice because you have been in dire situations before, and came through, seeing a brighter day. A friend I know counseled someone about their problems. She told them to just throw their hands up and start saying, *Hallelujah, hallelujah, hallelujah!* Guess what folks, you can't do that unless you truly trust God. It's His spirit that gives you hope and confidence that He will bring you through.

Are you currently feeling like you're in the middle of a storm and you're wondering what can possibly come next? If you're not feeling this now, you either have already, or you will in the future. Only God can see the true and full picture of our lives and situations. Take this time to think about if you truly trust God in times of confusion or if you rely on yourself or others more when the going gets tough. On the next page, write out all your worries and give them to God in prayer. He wants to carry your burdens.

I Am Covered by His Blood

And they overcame him by the blood of the Lamb, and by the word of their testimony; and they loved not their lives unto the death.
Revelation 12:11   KJV

Faithful believers know what the blood of the Lamb has done for their lives. So when trials, storms, and troubles blow in like a hurricane into their lives, instead of giving up in fear they call out to God in their distress. And say, *"Cover me with your blood"*.

The blood of Jesus is our covering, our hope, and our protection. God is ever faithful, even when you don't feel it or see it, He is right there and He has you covered. It is always amazing when He lets you feel and know when the storm has passed.

The blood of Jesus shed for us at Calvary can be "applied" to your life and situations even today. The blood is not a "cover-all", it does not work that way. It is a covering that is applied by calling on the name of Jesus Christ.

Ask God to carry out His perfect will in your life, your family, and your circumstances. Ask God to cleanse you of any sin with the blood, and that it would be a protection over you or the areas or people for which you're praying.

There is wonder-working power in the blood of Jesus!

No One Ever Cared for Me Like Jesus

For I know the thoughts that I think toward you, saith the Lord, thoughts of peace, and not of evil, to give you an expected end.
Jeremiah 29:11   KJV

As I was caring for my grandchildren on their overnight stay at my home, I was being so kind. I attended to their every need, listening to them as they talked to me. If they expressed a desire, I fulfilled it. It warmed my heart that they trusted me and that they expressed their desire to be with me. I knew at their age they were still dependent on the love and care of others, yet, I was so glad they seemed comfortable and loved, warm on a cold night.

I began to realize my heavenly Father loved me much more than that. He enjoys being with me. He delights in me talking to Him, expressing my needs and trusting him to meet them, and watching as I realize the depth of His love for me. We sell ourselves short if we don't truly get to know our Heavenly Father and spend time with Him, trusting Him with our problems.

Take a break today and just simply talk to God. Thank Him for loving you. Praise Him for His mighty acts. Write out your thankfulness for God on the next page and make a plan to spend more time with Him each and every day.

Read the Fine Print

For which of you, intending to build a tower, sitteth not down first, and counteth the cost, whether he have sufficient to finish it? Lest haply, after he hath laid the foundation, and is not able to finish it, all that behold it begin to mock him.
Luke 14:28-29   KJV

My husband was taking me to airport for an early morning flight. We got down the interstate 20 miles, then he asked me a simple question: *"Do you have your billfold, with your identity to get on the plane?"*

Surely I did, or so I thought. After all, I always carry my identification card with me. Not today. What happened, and where did I lose it? We turned around and headed back home to see if we could locate it. I found it; it had fallen out of my purse into the pocket of my car door. We got back on the road, racing to the airport by now, trying to get me to my flight. It was very doubtful that I would arrive on time, yet I had hope.

I was almost to the airport and re-read my ticket, and for the first time I noticed it: 8:30 PM, not 8:30 AM.

Oh my! How did I miss such a small error that would make so much difference in my trip. I called and paid extra to change it to accommodate my time frame. I felt much concern that I had overlooked such an important detail.

I began to ponder this and asked God, *"How can this apply to my life on earth?"* I don't want to make these kinds of mistakes about the important issues of life, for example, my connection to Him. I don't want to overlook the details in my life that God considers important.

My prayer that day was something like this:

God, I don't want to just assume I know You and that You are pleased with me. Illuminate the things in my life that are important to You… the things that I may have overlooked. I don't want to live my whole life thinking I am Yours and You are mine, only to find out at the end that I overlooked some important requirements to win the prize of eternity with You.

Earthly details in fine-print can sometimes be missed. It's in these times that we are simply inconvenienced. However, on the great day of your return back to God, there will be no adjustments or arguments about the fine print. Knowing His word and His requirements is essential for a safe arrival to our final destination.

Pray the prayer above for yourself - mean it! When God brings something about your thoughts or lifestyle to your attention, don't become bitter or take offense to the ways of God. Instead, be thankful for the opportunity to make a course-correction on your journey. Don't assume for yourself that God is pleased with you. Ask Him for yourself and listen to what He says back. Reflect on this in writing on the next page.

It Happened in the Furnace

Behold, I have refined thee, but not with silver; I have chosen thee in the furnace of affliction.
Isaiah 48:10   KJV

Grace enables us to see the hand of God in all things, so we can bear them without murmuring or complaining.

Job lost his family, his wealth, and his good health, yet he consoled himself (Job 23:14). David suffered much from his family and enemies, yet was happy to say, "My times are in your hands." (Psalms 31:15)

How wonderful to know God arranges things that come to pass in this world. When we find ourselves in dark times, we must fall upon the words of our Lord:

> *What I am doing you don't understand now, but afterward you will understand. John 13:7*

"The people of God have the same need of affliction...
that our bodies have of medicine,
that fruit trees have of pruning,
that gold and silver have of the furnace,
that iron has of the file, and
that the child has of the rod of correction!"

-An excerpt from *The Furnace of Affliction* by William Nicholson and Milburn Cockrell.

Ask God to help you see, through the eyes of Grace, His fingerprints all over your life and your situations. Thank God for the furnace - for through the furnace comes refinement. Ask God to mold you into His image and desire for you and your life.

I Belong to the King

*Trust in the Lord with all thine heart;
and lean not unto thine own understanding.*
Proverbs 3:5   KJV

Rev. J.C. Cole was a man we greatly admired in our early days of evangelizing, and we were blessed by the opportunity to preach for him. He used to sing a song called, "I Belong to the King". The story goes, he would sing that while he was working on the assembly line in Akron, Ohio. One of his co-workers heard him and said, *"Cole you don't belong to the King, you belong to Ferris Tire and Rubber Company!"*. Bro. Cole said, *"That's where you're wrong, I'm just here to pay expenses."*

If you are a true child of God, that's how you feel. You are here on this earth to do the Lord's bidding, and the things you have to do in this world are just to pay expenses so you can accomplish what God wants out of you while you walk this earth. The Bible tells us *"to seek first the kingdom of God, and all these things shall be added unto you."* I have found that to be true in my own life. The more I seek to do His will, the more joy, peace, and contentment I gain, with God even adding in the extras that I desire. Not because I focus on them, but because he knows my whole heart. He delights to surprise me with things I have desired to have. When you seek Him with your whole heart, your desires will be pure, and God will be able to fulfill them.

Take stock of your desires. Make a list of them and evaluate what needs to change. Is your first desire to know, love, and serve God? Re-align your desires and priorities to line up with God first. Focus on seeking God above all else, then watch what He can do!

He Knew How to Treat Others

*But I say unto you, Love your enemies,
bless them that curse you, do good to them
that hate you, and pray for them
which despitefully use you, and persecute you;*
Matthew 5:44   KJV

A wonderful man in our church was leading service and he voiced that on his tombstone he wanted these words: *He knew how to treat others.*

That struck a chord in me. I want that said about me. When you treat others with kindness, love, patience, consideration, long-suffering, goodness, and gentleness, then God is shining through you! There is not much of that available in our 21st century world. We need these fruits so that others will be drawn to us. When they get close to us, then we can speak of the hope that we have within us.

Make this your prayer today: *"Lord, lead me to esteem others over myself."* Only through God will we have the resources to do this. Ask Him to work through you as you reach and connect with others, that because of your kindness, others may see and come to know Him. Pray God would help you in conversations and in all manners of speech to reflect Him, and that you may treat others how God intended. How can you make an intentional effort this week to do that?

Give Me a Miracle Mindset

*My soul, wait thou only upon God;
for my expectation is from Him.*
Psalm 62:5   KJV

When troubles or problems come into your mind, look to God, and respond with a miracle mindset. There has to be a problem to get your answer; there has to be a difficulty to have an answer. Keep your faith in God and have a miracle mindset.

Instead of having a "woe-is-me" style, thoughts that are rooted in worry and anxiety, try these instead:

>God is up to something!
>God can make a way out of no way!
>I can't wait to see how God works this out!
>You have a million ways to solve this problem!
>God, You are great, even in the middle of this issue!

On the following page, write out some other things you can say when you have thoughts that worry you or cause you to be unsettled in your mind. Refer back to this book, and these pages, next time you are facing any other thought that is distracting you from what God is doing in your life.

God is on your side!

The Love of Christ Compels Me

I am the vine, ye are the branches: He that abideth in me, and I in him, the same bringeth forth much fruit: for without me ye can do nothing.
John 15:5   KJV

Sometimes when someone offends me or hurts me with their actions and/or their words, I want to give it back or give them what they deserve. Or worse, just cut them out of my life or circle. However, God compels me to live like He did. Since I am seeking to be like Christ, I must remember that He died on a cross for people that didn't want him. He went to the cross for people that despised Him and what he stood for. Yet, He made a way for them, hoping that someday when they need a savior there would be a way of escape.

It's never easy to live like Christ. It's one of the hardest things you'll ever do. However, if someday that person comes back to you to apologize and you have left an avenue for them to come to God, it will all be worth it.

Today, pray this: *Lord help me be like you, it's not in me naturally. It only comes when I yield my life to you. Help me respond slowly, to avoid anger and retaliation. Help me respond in love, then bring my hurts or concerns to You in private. Don't let me be the reason someone walks away from You without a way back.* Reflect on how you can be more Christ-like in in your responses and interactions below. Call and make amends with someone if God is leading you to, after you spend time in prayer and reflection.

Sheltered in the Arms of God

*God is our refuge and strength,
a very present help in trouble.*
Psalm 46:1   KJV

As the world waxes worse and worse, you hear of wars and rumors of war, and trouble on every corner. Living in the flesh will cause you to start having fearful thoughts: *"What if this happens, what if that happens?"*

As I was pondering the what ifs of my life one day, a song came on the radio station I was playing: *Sheltered in the Arms of God* by Dottie Rambo and Jimmie Davis. I use to sing this song.

*I feel the touch of hands so kind and tender
They're leading me in paths that I must trod
I have no fear when Jesus walks beside me
For I'm sheltered in the Arms of God*

*So let the storms rage high, the dark clouds rise
They won't worry me
For I'm sheltered safe within the arms of God
He walks with me and naught of earth shall harm me
For I'm sheltered in the arms of God*

*Soon I shall hear the call from Heaven's portal
"Come home my child It's the last mile you must trod"
I'll fall asleep and wake in God's new heaven
Sheltered safe within the arms of God*

We all can fall victim to the what-ifs of our lives. Instead of asking yourself, "What if?", tell God, "Even if... I will trust You!" Write your worries down as even-if statements below and let God handle them.

It's Possible With God

And he said, The things which are impossible with men are possible with God.
Luke 18:27   KJV

I love knowing that my God has the answer to all the things in my life that I have no answer to. Miracles happen everyday for those that believe He is able. When those miracles happen, I rejoice in the blessing of serving a prayer answering God. I rejoice knowing I don't have to do life alone. I have a caring and loving God walking each step with me. I can call on Him and ask anything, then trust that He will give me the best thing for my life.

Although sometimes I can only find one solution to my problem, God has a million ways to answer my needs. Your impossibility is God's opportunity to show up and show out in your life!

Keep believing and praying, because you never know what day your answer will come. Sometimes you need to stop and exclaim, *"It may happen today!"* What I had been praying for, the huge need in my life, the victory that I desired… It may happen when I least expected it to. One day you will say, *I fully believed God promised it and I knew it was going to happen. All of the sudden I realized today was the beginning of the fulfillment of my promise. It looked so hard to me, but God answered it so easily. We truly have an awesome God that knows the end from the beginning.*

What are you still waiting for God to accomplish in your life, or the life of a loved one? Write out praise and thanks to God for answering it, even though you can't see the answer right now.

Just and the Unjust

Many are the afflictions of the righteous: but the Lord delivereth him out of them all.
Psalm 34:19   KJV

Sometimes we feel that if we are a child of God who is serving Him to the best of our ability, then we should be exempt from troubles and afflictions. We know, however, that is simply untrue. God is glorified by the way we handle our problems with the help of His spirit within us.

I remember standing by my mother's bed as she was dying of cancer. My thoughts were, *God! Why is my mother suffering when she has walked with you all these years and helped so many people through their troubles and problems?* I have to admit I felt a twinge of bitterness, like God wasn't treating my mom fairly.

Just that quick, the Lord spoke to my spirit. *It happens to the just and the unjust alike.* God put me in my place, so to speak. How can we be a light to a dark world if God keeps us from all trials and tribulations? He gets glory when we honor Him in our actions and our faith in the midst of our troubles. Be assured if you are going through affliction, God will be there to comfort you. Through the trying of your faith, you will reap a blessed reward. You will have a testimony that will help someone else later in their walk with God. *"For you have been given not only the privilege of trusting in Christ but also the privilege of suffering for Him."* Philippians 1:29

Has God ever used you and the things you have been through to assist someone else on their journey? How did it make you feel? Continue to trust that He is with you through it all. Thank Him for his presence in your life.

_____

_____

_____

_____

_____

_____

_____

_____

_____

_____

_____

_____

_____

_____

_____

A Lion and a Pit

And Benaiah the son of Jehoiada, the son of a valiant man, of Kabzeel, who had done many acts, he slew two lionlike men of Moab: he went down also and slew a lion in the midst of a pit in time of snow: And he slew an Egyptian, a goodly man: and the Egyptian had a spear in his hand; but he went down to him with a staff, and plucked the spear out of the Egyptian's hand, and slew him with his own spear.
2 Samuel 23:20-21 KJV

I remember my husband preaching this sermon one Sunday and it was a message that resonated and stayed with me. I hadn't actually thought about it for a while, but one morning after my son was in a near-fatal car accident I woke up praying for him and the words "killing a lion in a pit on a snowy day" came to my mind. I knew that God was telling me something, that we would be fighting for my son's life and we would be fighting the worst kind of enemy, in the worst circumstance and in the worst kind of place.

We got the shocking call on a Saturday morning from our daughter-in-law. Marcus, our son, had been missing all night. He had left home at 5:00pm to get take-out for dinner. It was 8:30am when she called the next day and she still did not know where he was. She had called the police and filed a missing person report, they said they would check all the hospitals for her but there had been no news—no word at all. Our daughter-in-law sat home frantic with a six month old baby, no family nearby and no babysitter to call. There was no way that she could go out and look for him and she had no idea what had happened to our son.

When she called, I said "Let's pray. God will show us where he is."

We prayed and then after we hung up I called my daughter to tell her that her brother was missing. She felt impressed to call all the hospitals in Nashville. We called and the third hospital that we reached told us that Marcus was a patient there. He had been brought to the emergency room the day before, after a near-fatal car accident. Marcus had been hit by a drunk driver going 70 MPH, while he was turning into the restaurant parking lot.

This ordeal happened during the COVID-19 Pandemic on April 24-25, 2020. We knew that because of the restrictions put in place at hospitals due to the virus, that we would not be allowed to see our son or be with him. He would be fighting for his life with no loved ones beside him. I cried out to God and said, "I know You are with him." It felt like the worst scenario in every way. He was put on a ventilator and strapped to the bed to keep him from moving around and doing further damage to himself. All of this took place with no one there to be his advocate and his comfort.

The hospital provided the phone number to his nurse, and we were allowed to call for updates but it would be two weeks before we even knew what he looked like. Two nights after being admitted, he went off the ventilator and was moved to a step-down unit where they were able to feed him. Even though we had not been able to see him, we were encouraged that he was moving in the right direction. On the third night, though, I woke up praying for him. I knew something was happening and God wanted me to intercede for him. I prayed for quite awhile and then fell back to sleep. That morning when I woke up, the words "Killing a lion, in a pit, on a snowy day," rolled through my mind.

I knew that God was speaking to give me advance warning about what was coming next in our situation. While Marcus was in the step-down unit, they fed him not realizing that the ventilator had damaged the muscles needed for swallowing and the food was going into his lungs instead of his esophagus. He developed pneumonia, had to return to the ICU, and was put back on a ventilator.

People were praying for him worldwide and calling out to God to spare his life and heal him. God did spare his life and brought him back home in 26 days, without any needed surgeries. After having a feeding tube for 22 days, he passed a swallowing test and Marcus was able to eat and go home the next day. To God be the glory!!

When God shows you that you are up against the worst circumstance, the worst enemy, and the worst terrain to fight on, He is still able, more than able, to hear and answer prayer. To God be all the glory.

Reflect now on a time that you or someone you love felt all alone—fighting a lion in a pit on a snowy day. How did God rescue you or them? Thank Him for always being there, even in the worst possible scenarios that life puts us in.

While You're Waiting

Wait on the Lord: be of good courage, and He shall strengthen thine heart: wait, I say, on the Lord.
Psalm 27:14   KJV

When you were a child, it is likely that you felt that you simply could not wait. Not for the next holiday, the next snow day, the next age, the next vacation. You probably wanted everything that could happen, to happen. Waiting is not something that comes naturally to most of us. I believe we have all struggled with this at some point in our adult lives, too.

Have you ever tried to push God along in one way or another? Have you ever prayed about something, giving it to God, only to pick it back up and start running with it again after the answer didn't come when you wanted it to? That is not God's will for us or for our lives.

You must remember that in all situations, The Battle is the Lord's. While you wait, focus on prayer, reading the Word of God, and fasting. Read, pray, and reflect back on these devotions while you wait for God. Refer back to the things you have written every couple of months and look at the progress God has made in your life.

Thank you for joining me on this journey. May God bless you richly in your walk with Him.

Made in the USA
Monee, IL
23 October 2020